GROUNDBREAKERS

Charles Babbage

Neil Champion

Heinemann Library
Chicago, Illinois

© 2001 Reed Educational & Professional Publishing
Published by Heinemann Library,
an imprint of Reed Educational & Professional Publishing,
100 N. LaSalle, Suite 1010
Chicago, IL 60602
Customer Service 888-454-2279
Visit our website at www.heinemannlibrary.com

Designed by AMR
Originated by Ambassador Litho
Printed in Hong Kong/China

05 04 03 02 01
10 9 8 7 6 5 4 3 2 1

Library of Congress Cataloging-in-Publication Data

Champion, Neil.
    Charles Babbage / Neil Champion.
       p. cm. – (Groundbreakers)
    Summary: Examines the life and contributions of the English mathematician and inventor, whose work with calculating machines caused him to be called the father of the modern computer.
    ISBN 1-57572-367-0 (lib. bdg.)
    1. Babbage, Charles, 1791-1871—Juvenile literature. 2. Mathematicians—England—Biography—Juvenile literature. 3. Computers—History—Juvenile literature. [1. Babbage, Charles, 1791-1871. 2. Mathematicians. 3. Inventors.] I. Babbage, Charles, 1791-1871. II. Title. III. Series.

QA29.B2 C48 2000
510'.92—dc21
[B]   00-023384

Acknowledgments
The publishers would like to thank the following for permission to reproduce photographs:
By courtesy of the National Portrait Gallery, p. 4; National Gallery Picture Library, p. 6; Mary Evans Picture Library, pp. 7, 8, 10, 11, 13, 14, 18, 19, 30, 32, 34; Tate Picture Library, p. 9; AKG Photo London, p. 12; Science Photo Library, pp. 15, 20; Science and Society Picture Library, pp. 16, 22, 24, 26, 27, 28, 29, 31, 36, 37, 38, 40, 42; Bridgeman Art Library, pp. 17, 39; Roger Scruton, pp. 21, 41; Hulton Getty Picture Library, p. 23; Katz Pictures Ltd., p. 25; Corbis, p. 33; British Museum, p. 35; Royal Mail, p. 43.

Cover photograph reproduced with permission of the Science Photo Library.

Every effort has been made to contact copyright holders of any material reproduced in this book. Any omissions will be rectified in subsequent printings if notice is given to the publishers.

Some words are shown in bold, **like this.** You can find out what they mean by looking in the glossary.

Contents

Pioneer of the Computer

By 1845, Charles Babbage was hard at work on his Difference Engine.

Charles Babbage, who was born in 1791, was a man of great intellectual capacity and physical energy. He had a huge appetite for hard work and devoted himself to various activities during his long life. He was in turn a scientist, mathematician, inventor, philosopher, political and educational reformer, economist, and would-be politician—he failed in two attempts to get elected to the British Parliament. He was also a very sociable person, a gifted talker, and the founder of many clubs and societies. The task of classifying him is a hard one.

The computer pioneer

However, Babbage is best known today as a pioneer of the computer. He invented several calculating machines designed to process large numbers of mathematical calculations. People before him had seen how useful a system that could do this quickly might be and had devised various kinds of tables. Babbage took this search into the world of **precision engineering** and tried to develop a machine that would carry out the equations automatically, quickly, and with little or no error.

Babbage's special genius was to combine pure mathematical thought with the discoveries and advances gained from the **Industrial Revolution.** He not only wrestled with the theoretical problems of programming such machines, but he was also involved in their manufacture—the design, architecture, materials, and engineering problems that construction raised.

Applying science

This combination of science and engineering was a theme that occurred constantly in Babbage's ideas and work throughout his long life. We are used to seeing it around us today —in the manufacture of cars, jet fighters, medical machinery, and tools, and in computers themselves. In Babbage's time, however, the idea of applying mathematical thought to mechanical processes in a factory was revolutionary. This was his gift to the Victorian world.

Modern computers are a long way from Babbage's original idea.

We remember Babbage for his early work in computer science because of the computer's huge importance for us today. But he was also deeply involved in attempting to place science at the very heart of society and education, so that society—and, in particular, industry—could reap its benefits. Strangely enough, he met with a huge amount of resistance, from politicians and members of the ruling classes—though rarely from the industrialists. To understand the reason for this, we will need to look a little more closely at the society into which Babbage was born.

ONGOING IMPACT | **Science and mechanics**

Charles Babbage's unique contribution to science and mechanics was recognized by some of his contemporaries. Shortly after his death in 1871, Joseph Henry, secretary of the **Smithsonian Institutution,** wrote: "He more, perhaps, than any man who ever lived, narrowed the chasm [separating] science and practical mechanics."

Born at a Turning Point

Charles Babbage was born on December 26, 1791 at his parents' house on the Walworth Road, now part of south London, but his family roots lay in the southwest of England. His father, Benjamin Babbage, was a Devonshire banker, and his ancestors had been goldsmiths. The first record of the family dates from 1628, in the small town of Totnes. Charles's grandfather became **mayor** of Totnes in 1754. His mother, Elizabeth Plumleigh Teape, also came from an old Devonshire family. Several of her ancestors had also been mayors in Totnes. Both parents were from respectable, wealthy families.

The move to London

Benjamin and Elizabeth were married in Totnes in about 1790. A year later they moved to London, where Benjamin could be closer to his banking business. Charles was their first child. They had two more sons—Henry, born in 1794, and another Henry, born in 1796—but both died in childhood. A daughter, Mary Anne, born in 1798, survived into adulthood.

Babbage's England

England at the time of Babbage's birth was essentially rural—life went on in the fields and farms as it had for hundreds of years. Society consisted mainly of the land-owning **aristocrats** and the gentry (lesser landowners), small farmers, and agricultural workers. Domestic handicrafts, such as spinning wool, woodworking, and making cloth, supplemented the income of many. Small **cottage industries** existed in the villages and towns across the country.

This painting, The Haywain *by John Constable (1776–1837), shows the rural English landscape at the time of Babbage's birth. Steam power, railroads, and factories would soon change it forever.*

All forms of communication took time—roads were rough, and people traveled in carriages, on carts, on horseback, or on foot. Canals would soon become an important way of moving goods around the country, but not until the very end of the 18th century. Railroads would not appear until the 1830s. News and change traveled slowly.

*Before the **Industrial Revolution**, many farming families added to their income by activities such as spinning and weaving, which they carried out at home. This late 18th-century engraving shows women spinning, boiling yarn, and winding the yarn into reels.*

Change begins

Within a generation, this slow-paced country would change with a speed that astonished those, like Charles Babbage, who lived through the period. A revolution in agricultural methods improved production and increased the amount produced. Due partly to the **Enclosure Acts,** farms became larger and more efficient, but fewer in number. Rural communities lost their **common land.** And cottage industries declined due to competition from growing factories.

Charles Babbage was actively involved in the scientific developments that would move England forward into political reform, industrialization, and global trade. His life reflects the larger movements of the society he was part of.

Babbage's Early Years

As the son of a wealthy family in the early 1800s, young Charles Babbage would have gone to a school much like this one.

The young Charles went to school in London for a while, but he fell ill with a fever at the age of eight or nine and was sent to Devon to recover. His education continued at Alphington, where the boarding school he attended gave boys from wealthy families "instruction in English, Latin, and Greek languages." There is no mention of science and, as we shall see, later in his life Charles worked to have science more widely taught in schools. When he recovered his health, he was sent to a school in Enfield, which is now part of North London.

In Babbage's words:

"Amongst the books [in the school library] was a treatise on Algebra, called Ward's Young Mathematician's Guide. I was always partial to my arithmetical lessons, and this book attracted my particular attention. After I had been at this school for about a twelvemonth, I proposed to one of my school-fellows…that we should get up every morning at three o'clock…and work until five or half-past five. We accomplished this pretty regularly for several months."

Discovering mathematics

Charles took to mathematics and science early in life. He was an unusually gifted young student with a clever, inquiring mind.

Birth of a scientist

Charles's inventive mind was extremely active from an early age. An example of this was his attempt to build a simple machine that would allow him to walk on water. He attached two hinged wooden boards to his shoes.

In Babbage's words:

"I now went down to the river, and thus prepared, walked into the water...I now tried the grand experiment..."

He nearly drowned!

Leisure time

Charles spent a lot of his childhood vacations in Devon with his family and relatives. Here he enjoyed an active life in the country, away from his schoolwork. The young scientist was also a good swimmer, and he enjoyed hunting, fishing, and sailing.

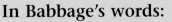

This view of Totnes, Devon, from the River Dart, was painted by J.M.W. Turner (1775–1851), one of the most famous British artists. Charles Babbage enjoyed his childhood vacations in Devon.

In Babbage's words:

"The grounds surrounding my father's house, near Teignmouth, extended to the sea. The cliffs, though lofty, admitted at one point of a descent to the beach, of which I very frequently availed myself for the purpose of bathing. One Christmas when I was about sixteen I determined to see if I could manage a gun. I accordingly took my father's fowling-piece, and climbing with it down to the beach, I began to look about for the large sea-birds which I thought I might have a chance of hitting."

The Industrial Revolution

Babbage was born into a world that was already beginning to change. Throughout the 18th century, new mechanical inventions changed the way tasks were carried out in agriculture, mining, and the textile industries. Mechanization slowly started to have an impact on the way people carried out their day-to-day work.

The first factory

In 1765 a new type of business had been set up in Soho, Birmingham, by Matthew Boulton, who described it as: "A noble range of manufactures…with connecting workshops sufficiently extensive for the accommodation of 1,000 workers… All the best machines and newest mechanical contrivances to save labour and perfect workmanship."

These were the first "manufactories"—soon known as factories. In the 19th century, the factory system changed the way goods were produced, the prices they were sold for, and the way people worked.

A change of pace

The pace of change increased in the 1780s and '90s, around the time of Charles's birth. New machinery began to make a real difference in the way people worked and lived.

In the words of the poet William Wordsworth:

"…the way people got on together in society was no longer important. Everything has been put up to market and sold for the highest price it would buy."

(In a letter written in 1817)

*Sheffield was one of the towns that grew very rapidly during the **Industrial Revolution.** It became a busy, crowded, and dirty center of manufacturing.*

The Industrial Revolution

The factory process was here to stay, as was the **market economy** that the poet Wordsworth described. It was efficient and highly profitable for the owners, the new **capitalists.** At this time, labor was cheap and there were few taxes, so factory owners could make huge fortunes. Manufacturing towns, such as Nottingham, Sheffield, and Birmingham, doubled or tripled in size during the 19th century. Canals helped with the distribution of goods and materials. The building of railroads from the 1830s onwards revolutionized communications and distribution.

This engraving shows the working conditions in a wool mill in the north of England at the time of the Industrial Revolution.

England was changing so much it was barely recognizable. People who had been pushed off the land during the **Agricultural Revolution** flooded into the towns to find work in the new factories. These workers became the new urban poor. At the same time, another new social class—the middle class— emerged. The new middle class controlled much of the country's wealth, and it also gained real political power after the **Great Reform Bill** of 1832. The population as a whole continued to grow, as advances in hygiene and medicine meant that more infants survived into adulthood and more adults lived longer.

Influences from France

Another major event that shaped the world in which Charles Babbage grew up was the French Revolution. This violent event erupted in 1789, stunning Europe and changing the course of European history.

France was the richest and most powerful country in Europe. During the 18th century, however, the French people became increasingly discontented with their king, and with the **aristocrats,** who were becoming more and more corrupt. Pressure grew to reform the **monarchy** and limit its power.

The Revolution begins

Events came to a head in May of 1789, when King Louis XVI tried to increase taxes. Representatives from the aristocrats, the church, and the commoners met to try to reform the **constitution** and control the excesses of the monarch. But disagreement among the three groups led to the formation of the National Assembly by the commoners in June 1789. Then on July 14, a crowd of ordinary Parisians, angry at the high price of bread, marched on the Bastille prison and freed the prisoners. The Revolution had started.

This painting was made during the French Revolution. It shows the storming of the Bastille prison on July 14, 1789. This event, which came to symbolize the Revolution, is still celebrated in France every year by a national holiday—Bastille Day.

The Reign of Terror

France was now ruled by the National Assembly. The new government set out to bring *"Liberté, égalité, et fraternité"* (liberty, equality, and brotherhood) to the people. At first it tried to create a **constitutional monarchy,** but a few years later France was declared a **republic,** and the king and many aristocrats were executed. The **guillotine** was invented specifically for the purpose of swift, efficient beheading. The Revolution now fell into the hands of extremists, and a so-called Reign of Terror followed, when thousands of "enemies of the Revolution" died at the guillotine.

Babbage and the Revolution

Babbage was in favor of reform and progress. His ideas were a version of those behind the French Revolution. Politics in 19th-century England were defined by these ideas. People either stood up against them or were in favor of them to varying degrees. They could not be ignored. Babbage disapproved of the bloodshed and extreme politics that were practiced by some of the revolutionaries. But he believed in the new **capitalism** and industrialization that flourished around him, and he saw that greater freedom could help them develop.

The books of the French philosopher and writer Jean-Jacques Rousseau (1712–78) had a strong influence on the French Revolution. One of them, The Social Contract (1762), emphasized the rights of the people over those of the government.

NAPOLEON BONAPARTE

As the Revolution unfolded in France, much of the rest of Europe, especially the kings, queens, and aristocrats, watched in horror, terrified that the new ideas would spread. France's neighbors—Austria, Prussia, and Britain—declared war on France. A brilliant young soldier came forward in France's defence. His name was Napoleon Bonaparte and his rise to power was swift. By 1799 he was ruler of his country. Wars continued until Napoleon was finally defeated in 1815. The Revolution was over. But the world had had a taste of revolution—of ordinary working people having their day—that it would not forget.

Cambridge and the Analytical Society

In 1810, Charles Babbage began his studies at Cambridge University. The atmosphere was very formal, and students were required to wear gowns.

In October 1810, at the age of 19, Babbage entered Trinity College at Cambridge University to study mathematics and chemistry. His views on politics, reform, **liberalism,** and the state of science in his country were all formed during this period, and so were some important and lasting friendships with influential people.

He was, however, extremely disappointed with the way mathematics was taught at the university. He went there with high hopes, but quickly realized that the standard of teachers was very low. All the important work in scientific investigation and mathematics was going on in continental Europe. At least at Cambridge he had access to a library that contained books and papers from the academies of Paris and Berlin.

Expanding interests
As well as pursuing his mathematical studies, Babbage threw himself into the social side of university life. He enjoyed the company of men with similar interests and became a popular person. He spent time playing chess and cards and sailing on the River Cam, and stayed up late in discussion with friends.

Babbage had an allowance from his father of £300 a year, a very good income for a young man in the early 19th century. He kept records of what he spent his money on. This included wine, dances, a dog, trips to London, books for his studies, and instruments for chemistry experiments.

The Analytical Society

To make up for his disappointment with Cambridge intellectual life, Babbage helped set up a society dedicated to science. It was called the Analytical Society and was made up of other students at the university with similar interests and opinions. The main members were John Herschel (its first president), Alexander D'Arblay, Edward Ryan, Sir Edward Ffrench Bromhead, and George Peacock. The intense discussions and the friendships Charles made through the Analytics remained lasting influences throughout his long life. Many of the plans and ideas that he worked on in later years were hatched in debate with his friends at meetings of this society.

Trinity College, where Babbage studied, had been Isaac Newton's college, and the memories of that great scientist were everywhere. However, it was generally accepted that standards of scientific study had fallen since their high point under Newton in the 17th century. Babbage realized this, and changing the situation became one of his most important goals. He became one of England's leading supporters of scientific reform and campaigned throughout his life to return science and scientists to the high status that they had once held.

John Herschel (1792–1871), an astronomer, chemist, and photographer, was one of England's greatest scientists. He met Babbage at Cambridge, where they were both founding members of the Analytical Society. They remained friends, and Babbage named one of his sons after Herschel.

15

Married Life

Georgiana Whitmore instantly captivated Charles Babbage.

Babbage probably first met Georgiana Whitmore in Teignmouth in Devon during his first summer vacation from Cambridge in 1811. Her family came from Dudmaston in Shropshire, in the English Midlands. The couple got married on July 2, 1814, shortly after Charles finished at Cambridge. They spent their honeymoon in Devon, at a farm near the pretty village of Chudleigh. Most of their married life was spent in London, where they had eight children. It was a very close and supportive marriage.

However, Charles's father did not approve of the marriage. Charles had not yet made a mark upon the world or found a means of earning an income. Benjamin Babbage had retired from banking in 1803 and had gone back to Devon. His views were old-fashioned, and his harsh attitude toward the marriage caused a rift with his son that lasted until Benjamin's death in 1827.

Finding a role in life

When he first fell in love, Charles decided that a career in the church would provide the security and income he needed to raise a family. However, even before the wedding he had decided against this idea. He then thought of following his father into banking. This idea was also dropped, although he did become involved in the insurance business for a short time later in life. He had a small income from his father of £450 a year—a comfortable amount, but not enough to make him rich.

Middle-class families like the Babbages could afford to raise their children in relative luxury and send them to good schools.

In the autumn of 1815 Charles and Georgiana moved into a small house in Devonshire Street in London, which would become their family home. The question of what he was to do with his life and how he would earn his living was still unanswered. Georgiana did not put pressure on him, and was supportive of all his ideas. He began a series of lectures on astronomy for the **Royal Institution,** and within a few years he had established himself firmly in the scientific community in London. Now he was ready to pursue scientific reform.

INFANT MORTALITY

Babbage was one of four children, but two of his brothers died in infancy. He and Georgiana had eight children between 1815 and 1827. However, only three of them lived into adulthood—Herschel, Dugald, and Henry. These terrible statistics were by no means unusual in the early 19th century. Advances in childcare, hygiene, and medicine meant that children's survival rates improved considerably as the century progressed. This was one of the main reasons for the huge growth in population that followed.

The Scientific Tradition

To understand the concerns that Babbage had about the state of science in his country a little better, it is helpful to look at the scientific tradition as it had developed in England by the early 19th century. Only then does the influence that Babbage had on the development of science become clear.

Scientific influences

Francis Bacon (1561–1626) was one of the first men to realize how important it was to carry out a scientific method when making experiments and recording the results. In a book called *The Advancement of Learning* (1605), Bacon showed that through the scientific discovery of facts about the natural world, people could increase their power and influence over the environment. In a similar way, Babbage fought to apply scientific method to the great industrial problems of his day. The **Industrial Revolution** had been started by ordinary men without the help of high science, but Babbage saw what advantages there could be if this were to change.

Sir Francis Bacon (1561–1626) was an English writer, philosopher, and politician. Although Bacon was not a scientist, he helped to establish the methods of scientific research that are still used today.

Sir Isaac Newton (1642–1727) was one of the most famous mathematicians the world has known. He discovered the laws of **gravity,** split white light into its many colors, developed his three famous **laws of motion,** and devised **calculus.** He was elected a fellow of the **Royal Society** in 1672 and became its president in 1703. Newton's influence on the scientific community was enormous. He was knighted for his services in 1705, and when he died he was buried in Westminster Abbey. Babbage looked to this period as the Golden Age of science in England—scientists were then held in high esteem.

Sir Isaac Newton (1642–1727), is famous for discovering the laws of gravity, but his contributions to science covered a huge range of topics. Newton had been a member of Trinity College, Cambridge, where Babbage also studied.

The Decline of Science

After Newton, the situation changed. A lack of interest on the part of society, combined with an absence of great thinkers to follow Newton, was to blame. Babbage later wrote a book on the subject called *The Decline of Science* (1830), in which he blamed the Royal Society, the education system, indifference and snobbery on the part of the rich and powerful, and a lack of leadership. His book pointed out that it was all very different in the rest of Europe, where cooperation between practical men of industry and scientists was encouraged, not looked down on.

In John Herschel's words:

"Here, whole branches of continental discovery are unstudied …we are fast dropping behind. In mathematics we have long since drawn the rein, and given over a hopeless race. In chemistry the case is not much better."

Babbage and the Royal Society

Sir Joseph Banks (1743–1820), who was president of the Royal Society from 1778 until his death, disagreed with Babbage's ideas about science.

The **Royal Society** is the oldest and one of the most important scientific societies in Britain. It was formed in 1645 to provide a forum for the greatest minds of the day to discuss scientific and mathematical problems. Some of its first members included Sir Christopher Wren, the architect who designed St. Paul's Cathedral in London; Robert Boyle, the Irish chemist and physicist; Abraham Cowley, the poet and scientist; and Bishop Thomas Sprat.

One of the early goals of the Society was to bring together all branches of the developing sciences and knowledge in general under a single banner. Its members, called fellows, came from a variety of backgrounds. Sir Isaac Newton was elected a fellow in 1672 and made president in 1703. The Society at this time was composed of well-educated men, many of whom were **aristocrats.** What bound them together was their active interest in furthering human knowledge through experiment and writing.

Decline of the Society

However, by Babbage's time, the Royal Society was no longer a gathering for outstanding scientists. It had become a club for aristocrats who liked to dabble in science, but in reality were contributing very little to finding out new things about the world around them. Babbage saw its deterioration as a symbol of the greater decline of science in general in Britain.

He became a member in 1816 and tried to get a reformer—his friend John Herschel—elected president. He wanted the Society completely overhauled and brought back to its original principles. This was not a popular move and was resisted by the powerful men who ran the Society.

Rival societies

Babbage also wanted to see other societies formed that would focus on more specific branches of the sciences. The president of the Royal Society at that time, Sir Joseph Banks, did not like the idea. He thought that the foundation of other societies would undermine the importance and power of the Royal Society, so he actively tried to keep them from being formed. However, he was not successful.

The Cambridge Philosophical Society (founded in 1819 by former members of the Analytical Society), the Geological Society, and the Astronomical Society (founded in 1820 by Babbage, Herschel, and others) all came into existence to meet the growing needs of serious scientists like Babbage. Times and attitudes were changing. Babbage was in tune with the new thinking, while Sir Joseph Banks and the Royal Society were not. But the Royal Society still had a great deal of influence in the highest social circles in England.

The Royal Society building in London was not far from the Geological Society offices.

Applied Science

Babbage truly believed that science could be a huge benefit to industry in an increasingly competitive world. The **Industrial Revolution** had started with no help from the government, universities, or any other established institution. It was driven by practical men who found solutions to the problems of producing goods faster and more efficiently. One such person was Richard Arkwright (1732–92), who invented the spinning frame and many other machines that speeded up the manufacture of textiles, and who had himself received little formal education.

As the years went by, production became increasingly sophisticated, as did the machinery that made it possible. The problems that industry faced needed people like Babbage to help solve them. This was happening in countries like Germany and France, and Britain was losing first place in world trade and development to these countries.

In Richard Arkwright's words:

"It is well known that the most useful discoveries that have been made in every branch of art and manufacture have not been made by speculative philosophers in their closets, but by ingenious mechanics."

Babbage received this diploma from the Academy of Sciences, Arts, and Humanities in Dijon, France.

Visiting factories

Babbage made a point of visiting factories and other places of manufacture. For example, he went on a tour of England and Scotland in 1823, financing himself out of his own private income. Accompanied by Georgiana, he visited industrialists and mill owners. He showed great understanding of the day-to-day problems of running a factory.

Solving problems

Babbage saw the need, for example, to store energy created by the very powerful source of harnessed steam. If this could be stored, then factories could work for longer. Babbage also saw that the French metric system, introduced under Napoleon, was a logical way to measure and weigh things. He fought to have it instituted in Britain, but he failed. It was 100 years before the system began to be used in Britain.

In 1832 Babbage published his thoughts concerning the state of industry and commerce in *On the Economy of Machinery and Manufactures*. In this book his unique talent of combining science with an excellent understanding of the problems of industry really came to the surface. His book was the product of hundreds of visits to factories and other places of manufacture. It was an instant success, selling 3,000 copies as soon as it was published. It was translated into French and German in 1833 and later into Italian. However, in England its important message of applying science and technology to the problems of industry was ignored in practice.

The Rocket, *the **steam locomotive** built by George Stephenson and his son Robert in 1829, ran from Liverpool to Manchester. It marked the beginning of the age of the railroad, another development during the Industrial Revolution.*

Mathematical Tables

The project that would last the rest of Babbage's life started with the idea of eliminating error from the production of mathematical tables by using calculating machines rather than humans to work on them. These machines—the Difference Engines and the Analytical Engine—were to become his obsessive projects. But why were tables of numbers so important at the time?

Errors in production

Printed tables of numbers had been in existence for a few hundred years. They were used by scientists, navigators, engineers, surveyors, and bankers to make instant calculations. They took a long time to produce and were a lot of work. The results were generally full of errors. Errors crept in at three stages: in making calculations, in copying the results, and in typesetting and printing the volumes of tables. A random selection of 40 volumes of tables looked at in 1834 had 3,700 mistakes! Babbage himself worked on a set of tables and owned one of the largest collections—over 300 volumes. Errors in the tables could result in enormous cost to the user. For example, Babbage calculated that the government lost 2 to 3 million pounds every year due to errors in tables used to calculate **annuities.** In other areas the cost could be in lives as well as in money.

Babbage collected books of mathematical tables, some of which are shown here.

Shipwrecks were common in Babbage's time, and many people died as a result of them. Babbage wanted to change all that by providing accurate navigation tables.

"The safety of the tens of thousands of ships upon the ocean, the accuracy of coast surveys, the exact position of light-houses, the track of every shore from headland to headland, the latitude and longitude of mid-sea islands, the course and motion of currents, direction and speed of winds,...in short, everything which constitutes the chief element of international commerce in modern times, depends upon the fullness and accuracy of tables."

(Joseph Henry, Report of the **Smithsonian Institution**, 1873)

Navigation tables

Britain was the greatest seafaring nation of the early 19th century. Its wealth depended upon the success of its merchant ships trading around the globe. But shipping tables used for navigation were full of errors, which often caused shipwrecks. One of the main reasons for developing a calculating machine was to produce accurate tables for the navy. The government therefore gave money to Babbage to start work on the project.

In Babbage's words:

"The first idea which I remember of the possibility of calculating tables by machinery occurred in the year 1820 or 1821: it rose out of the following circumstances. The Astronomical Society had appointed a committee consisting of Sir J. Herschel and myself to prepare certain tables; we had decided on the proper formulae and had put them in the hands of two computers [people hired to do calculations] for the purpose of calculation. We met one evening for the purpose of comparing the calculated results, and finding many discordancies, I expressed to my friend the wish, that we could calculate by steam..."

Steps Towards a Computer

Babbage started work on designing calculating engines in 1821. He was to spend much of the rest of his life, some 50 years, working on them. They were constantly woven into whatever else he was doing. It is important to understand that his machines were designed to be made out of metal. None was ever completed, but had they been, they would have filled an entire room and weighed several tons. They would not have looked anything like the machine we call a computer today.

What is a computer?

Today we take computers for granted. They have been around for decades. They are advertised everywhere and are now found in virtually all workplaces, schools, and colleges, and in many homes, at least in the developed world. They are constantly being improved, and with the coming of the Internet, they are beginning to dominate the world of communication and information.

But what is the definition of the term "computer?" At its simplest, it means a machine that can compute or calculate numerical data that is fed into it. Their development is rooted in 20th-century technology, but they have a history that goes back a lot further than that. Babbage, as we have seen, is known as a pioneer of the computer. But even he took the idea of a machine that could handle large complex sums from others who came before him.

Blaise Pascal (1623–62), the French philosopher and mathematician, built this calculating machine between 1642 and 1644, when he was about 19, to help his father with his business. It could add and subtract.

Early experiments

The ancient Greeks had experimented with making calculating machines. But it was not until the 17th century that technological advances in materials and design enabled calculators to become a real possibility. The first calculating machine was made by a man named Wilhelm Schickard. He called it a

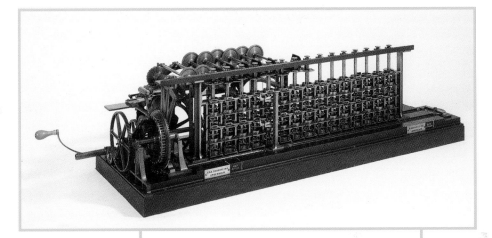

A Swedish father-and-son team, Georg and Edvard Scheutz, developed and built several versions of their Difference Engine.

calculating clock and made it out of wood. The French philosopher Blaise Pascal made and sold simple calculating machines in the 1640s. In England in the 1660s a man named Samuel Morland overcame one of the problems early designers had come across: that of carrying numbers over from the units column to the tens and on to the hundreds. He added an extra set of wheels to store the numbers on. The user then had to take them over manually.

Contemporary efforts

The German mathematician Johann Müller (1746–1830) was the first person to discuss a printing calculator that would use the mathematical principle of addition or finite differences. His work was known to Babbage, who translated some of it from the German. A father-and-son team from Sweden, Georg and Edvard Scheutz, used Babbage's own work to help them. However, their efforts ended in failure and they died bankrupt and unnoticed. Other people who tried to develop calculating machines in the 19th century included Martin Wiberg in Sweden and Barnard Grant in the United States. Like Babbage's efforts, their attempts were unsuccessful.

Building the Difference Engine

Babbage started off making parts of the calculating machine himself. These included cardboard cut-outs and sketches. He actually had a **lathe** of his own and had made some advances using it. But it was too limited a tool—he needed help. At first this was achieved by sending out designs to different workmen and then assembling the pieces himself. He was afraid that his ideas might be stolen by somebody else, so this method helped keep the overall plan secret. By 1822 he already had a model version. It was this that he used to secure government finance. Once that was in place, he could employ the skilled labor he needed to get the project really under way.

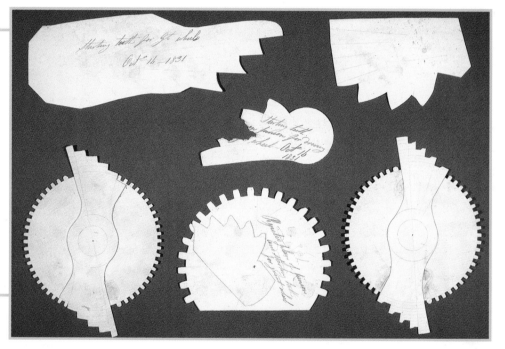

While working on the first version of his calculating machine, Babbage made cardboard cut-outs of its components to see how it would work when put together.

Error-free calculations

The biggest difference between the earlier machines and the ones that Babbage worked on was that the earlier ones needed the operator to interact with them continually. This made them slow and open to human error. Babbage realized that one of the potential strengths of using a machine to carry out large calculations was that the results would be free of error. In a sense, what he wanted to do was apply the factory system to calculations—mechanizing the process and, in doing so, removing human error and inefficiency. Machines are far better than humans at doing repetitive, complex tasks.

He approached the government for financial help with developing his ideas for such a calculating machine. He had a meeting in 1823 with the **Chancellor of the Exchequer** that ended in success. He was given the sum of £1500 (a small fortune) to continue work on the project.

If the first Difference Engine had ever been completed, it would have been enormous. It would have been 8 feet (2.4 meters) high, 7 feet (2.1 meters) long and almost 3 feet (1 meter) wide. With 25,000 separate parts, it would have weighed several tons. The portion that was finally built had over 2,000 working parts.

The engine would be made of metal (cast iron, bronze, and steel) beautifully constructed by skilled craftsmen using the most up-to-date precision tools of the day. It would consist of columns of wheels with numbers for units, tens, hundreds, and so on. These would be activated by a system of gears, **cams,** levers, and racks. A model of the partially-constructed machine, from 1832, is on display at the Science Museum in London. Babbage's plan was for it to have a 20-decimal capacity, and so be able to produce tables consisting of huge figures. Like all his calculating machines, the first Difference Engine—the name he gave to his automatic calculating machine—was never finished.

Skilled engineers

Babbage employed a skilled engineer, Joseph Clement, to help work on building his first Difference Engine. A side benefit of the project was that Clement's workshop, funded partly by the money coming in to build the calculating engine, became a center for the development of precision machine tools. The men he hired to help with the project became instrumental in the growth and direction of light engineering in England at this time. However, Babbage later argued with Clement over money, an event that marked the end of work on the engine.

Part of the first Difference Engine was built in 1832 by engineer Joseph Clement, following Babbage's designs.

The Working Machine

How exactly would the Difference Engine produce the mathematical tables? Basic mathematics works on the principles of addition, subtraction, multiplication, and division. People quickly realized that addition and subtraction were much easier to mechanize than multiplication and division. It was also easier to pick up on any errors in the calculations. Therefore, Babbage designed the Difference Engine to work by calculating tables through additions.

The operator would input the calculations and set the machine up, then turn a cranking handle. This would set the wheels and cogs in motion to produce and automatically print the results in the form of tables of numbers.

In Babbage's words:

"It is important to state distinctly at the outset, that the Difference Engine is not intended to answer special questions. Its object is to calculate and print a series of results called Tables—many such are in use in various trades. For examples— there are collections of Tables of the amount of any number of pounds from 1 to 100 lbs of butchers' meat at various prices per lb."

"The marvellous pulp and fibre of a brain had been substituted by brass and iron, he had taught wheelwork to think."

(A description of a Babbage engine in the 1870s)

The Duke of Wellington was one of the powerful **aristocrats** who came to see the first Difference Engine at Babbage's home in Dorset Street in London.

The second Difference Engine was finally built in 1991 by engineers at the Science Museum in London. It was part of the celebration of the 200th anniversary of of Babbage's birth.

Unfinished engines

Babbage's machines were never fully completed. He abandoned the first Difference Engine in 1833. He never built the second or the third, although extensive work was done on them in the 1840s. His work on a different type of machine, the Analytical Engine, ended the same way. There are many reasons why Babbage did not complete the machines. They include increased costs and time, political hostility, disagreement with engineers, and the lack of special tools to make the pieces at the time.

ONGOING IMPACT   Machine tools

Perhaps one of the most valuable and lasting contributions to society that came out of all the work and effort on the calculating machines was that of advancing the techniques used to make precision tools. Engineers found practical ways to make high-quality and very accurate metal tools for making parts of the engines. The craftsmanship involved was used in other engineering projects from the mid-19th century onwards.

Tragedy and Travel

Paris in 1816 was home to a thriving scientific community.

In 1819, four years after the end of the Napoleonic wars against France, Babbage had made his first trip to Paris, with his friend John Herschel. They had met many important members of the scientific community in the city. These included Pierre-Simon de Laplace (1749–1827) and Claude Louis Berthollet (1748–1822), a chemist. Both men were involved with applying science to practical problems in industry. Babbage had found that the French education system had adopted the idea of the *écoles polytechniques*, specialist colleges that trained highly skilled craftsmen and technicians who went on to work in the new industries of their country. No such system existed in England, where the rich studied Greek, Latin, and law, and the poor were hardly educated at all.

Death of Georgiana

The year of 1827 was a bad one for Charles Babbage. His father died in February, at the age of 74. But worse was to come. Charles's wife Georgiana died in August 1827. They had been a very close couple, and he was utterly devastated. He went to stay in Slough in Berkshire at the house of his friend, John Herschel.

The Babbages' young son, Charles, had died just before his mother, in July 1827, and a newly-born son also died with his mother. All in all, this was a dreadful time for the 36-year-old Babbage.

Charles's mother was very worried about him after Georgiana died. She contacted John Herschel for news of Charles, and wrote in response to him:

"You give me great comfort in respect to my son's bodily health. I cannot expect the mind's composure will make hasty advance. His love was too strong and the dear object of it too deserving..."

Travels in Europe

Babbage left England to travel again in Europe shortly after this tragedy, and he remained away for over a year. He left his oldest son Herschel and his daughter Georgiana with his mother, who was living in London. His other two sons, Dugald and Henry, went to stay with their aunt and uncle. Part of his plan was to do a comprehensive survey of industry and technological advances in the countries he visited. His tour took him through the Netherlands, Germany, Austria, Italy, and France. He finally returned home late in 1828.

Pierre-Simon de Laplace was a French astronomer and mathematician. Babbage first met him in Paris in 1819.

Technology as our servant

While he was away, Babbage visited factories, met craftsmen, engineers, and scientists, and discussed problems that faced industry throughout Europe. These included, for example, how to increase markets for sales, how to improve output, new machinery, and training a workforce. He became convinced that through the use of machinery, and technology in general, the greater good of the human race would be served. He saw some of the misery and inequalities that the factory system produced, but he saw as clearly the very concrete benefits that it bestowed. Goods were cheap and more widely available, and producing them created employment.

Babbage also saw that Britain, the country that had started the process of industrialization, was rapidly losing ground to those very countries that he was currently visiting, especially France and the German states. More than ever he was convinced that something had to be done, and that a systematic approach to the application of science to industry should be central to the next phase of industrial development.

Babbage and Reform

Babbage ran for election to Parliament twice and would have given speeches at political gatherings like this one.

In many ways, Charles Babbage was a typical man of his generation. He was interested in many of the things that were going on around him and he actively involved himself in them. His sharp and critical mind allowed him to see shortcomings in whatever he was analyzing. He could often see how things might be done more efficiently. The desire to improve came naturally to him. And he was free from **bigotry** and petty nationalism, which meant that he did not look down on people or ideas just because they were not British. This viewpoint enabled him to question why Britain did not adopt the good ideas that came from other countries. In an age when everything French was looked upon with deep suspicion, Babbage was able to see the superiority of the decimal system, which had been adopted in France, and of the French education system.

In Babbage's words:

"It is…not unreasonable to suppose that some portion of the neglect of Science in England, may be attributed to the system of education we pursue."

Scientific reform

Closest to his heart was the reform of science in Britain. This concern began during his student days at Cambridge. He helped set up the Analytical Society in 1812 as a way of introducing European scientific and mathematical developments into Britain. Later he attacked the complacent scientific community in his book *Reflections on the Decline of Science in England, and on Some of its Causes* (1830). One of his main targets was the **Royal Society.**

Babbage was severely critical of the teaching in English private schools and universities, which concentrated on traditional subjects like Latin and Greek at the expense of science. He believed that the scorn for science and industry found in these schools were due to snobbery. But he also had plenty of ideas on how reform might improve the situation, and he made suggestions for educational and **curriculum** changes.

Political reform

Babbage tried to be elected to Parliament twice, in 1832 and 1834. On both occasions he ran in the **constituency** of Finsbury, in North London, and both times he lost. Political reform was in the air at this time. The **Great Reform Bill** of 1832 extended voting rights to all male householders of property worth £10 or more in cities, and widened the vote in the country. Unrepresentative and corrupt constituencies were abolished, and parliamentary seats were redistributed on a fairer basis. The expanding middle classes and the growing cities and towns benefited the most from these reforms.

Broadly speaking, Babbage supported reform. There were two political parties in Britain at the time: the Whigs and the Tories. It was the Whigs who supported the Reform Bill, after which they became known as the Liberal Party. Tories had been in power for decades. This was the Whigs' opportunity to re-establish political power, and they were expecting many of the middle classes to use their new vote in their favor.

This cartoon appeared in 1832, the year Babbage ran for election to Parliament for the first time. It shows the contradictions some people saw in the political ideas of the time—how could a country be a republic and have a king at the same time?

AN EXCELLENT REPUBLICAN KING.

The Analytical Engine

In 1834, one year after abandoning work on the first Difference Engine, Babbage started thinking about another type of engine. This one would be more powerful and complex than the Difference Engine, which was designed to produce and print tables of figures only. The Analytical Engine would be able to perform a variety of mathematical tasks. Babbage's title of "Father of the Computer" rests upon this new engine. In this same year, Babbage's only daughter, Georgiana, died. Once again, he was devastated by the loss.

The Analytical Engine—a computer?

The concept for the Analytical Engine has many things in common with the principles of a modern-day computer. It was to be programmable, in that it would use a series of punched cards to provide it with instructions. It would have a place where results could be stored, ready to be used in other equations. It would have a separate "mill" where the mathematical processing happened. It would be able to repeat a process any number of times, which could be programmed by the user. Babbage also considered building into it the ability to work on several calculations at the same time.

All these thought processes behind the development of the Analytical Engine make it part of the early history of computer development. However, there would be a gap of over 100 years between the idea of the Analytical Engine and the first steps towards a modern computer.

Babbage designed these punched cards to give information and instructions to his Analytical Engine.

Ada Lovelace, who became a close friend of Babbage, was the daughter of the poet Lord Byron. She was a gifted mathematician in her own right and translated from Italian an important essay on Babbage's calculating machine. She also worked on some of the programmed punch-cards, and has even been called the first computer programmer.

The design

Like all of Babbage's calculating engines, the Analytical Engine was never finished in his lifetime. This became a source of deep discontent for him. Many models and parts of the Engines were built, ranging from small cardboard models and sketches to the part of the first Difference Engine completed by 1833 and the portion of the mill of the Analytical Engine that existed at his death in 1871. The full Engine, had it been completed, would have been 15 feet (4.6 meters) high, 20 feet (6.1 meters) long, and 6 feet (1.8 meters) wide. It would have consisted of thousands of moving parts and weighed several tons.

In Ada Lovelace's words:

"[The Analytical Engine] is not a thinking being, but simply an automaton which acts according to the laws imposed upon it."

Government and the Engines

This detailed design drawing by Babbage shows wheels that would become part of the second Difference Engine.

Babbage worked on calculating engines of one sort or another throughout his life. They sat at the center of his mathematical and design goals. He took their failure to be completed very personally, as well as the failure of the government and various institutions to see their potential and back them. In 1862, when Babbage was 70, the working portion of his first Difference Engine was exhibited at the **International Exhibition** in London. But it was given a very small display. "English Engine Poked into a Hole" was the famous remark he made about it. He felt misunderstood and unrewarded by his country. In 1828 he was made Professor of Mathematics at Cambridge, but that was the sum of his recognition. He read about his appointment in a newspaper while traveling through Italy.

Financial support

Machines as huge and complex as the ones that Babbage designed were expensive to produce. It has been estimated that the first Difference Engine had cost the government £17,470 by the time work stopped on it in 1833. This was an enormous sum.

Many people believe that the advances in precision-tool engineering made by Babbage and the engineer Joseph Clement make the expense worthwhile, canceling out the disappointment for the overall failure to build a complete version. However, after the first Difference Engine, Babbage would never again get so much money. He ended up spending considerable sums of his own. "I have sacrificed time, health, and fortune, in the desire to complete these Calculating Engines," he said in 1852.

This sketch shows Sir Robert Peel, Prime Minister from 1834 to 1835 and again from 1841 to 1846, reading to Queen Victoria. He was not supportive of Babbage's work and he wondered, "What shall we do to get rid of Mr. Babbage and his calculating machine?"

Differing views:

*"Mr. Goulburn, **Chancellor of the Exchequer,** asked my opinion on the utility of Mr. Babbage's calculating machine, and the propriety of spending further money on it. I replied that it was worthless."*

(Sir George Airy, Astronomer Royal, 1842)

"Mr. Babbage's projects appear to be so indefinitely expensive, the ultimate success so problematical, and the expenditure certainly so large and so utterly incapable of being calculated, that the Government would not be justified in taking upon itself any further liability."

(The Chancellor of the Exchequer, 1852)

Other opinions paint a different picture. One minister said:

"I wrote to one of the most eminent mechanical engineers to enquire whether I should be safe in stating to the Government that the expense of the Calculating Engine had been more than repaid by the improvements in mechanism directly referable to it; he replied— unquestionably."

The Final Years

In 1860, at the age of 68, Charles Babbage attended the fourth International Statistical Congress.

Babbage's final years were a bit lonely. He never remarried after Georgiana died. He had a disagreement with his eldest son, Herschel, who in 1839 had married Laura Jones, a woman from a lower class and without a **dowry.** Babbage's behavior was very similar to that of his own father when he married Georgiana. Herschel became an engineering inspector. In November 1851 he and his family left England for Australia, where he worked for the Geological Survey.

Henry Babbage, the younger surviving son, entered the India Service and took up a military career in that country, leaving England in 1843. However, he did return to England in March 1871, and saw his dying father through his last weeks.

Babbage's mind was still active, and he was not the type of person to get depressed. The calculating engines had become so much a part of his life that, in old age, he simply could not stop working on them. He had learned the hard way the simple lesson that building one of his machines was an enormous undertaking, in terms of time and money. He set about reducing their complexity and working on ways to mass-produce some of the parts.

Battles with street noise

Babbage was never afraid to take on a cause that he felt was just. Dorset Street, where he lived in London, had become much busier and livelier over the years. A bar had opened, along with a taxi stand. Street noise became a real nuisance. Organ grinders, brass bands, fiddlers, and, he said, "troupes of Scotch imposters dancing with bagpipes, even more inharmonious than the genuine instrument" could be found playing for coins outside his window. He raised a Bill in Parliament that gave residents power to regulate the noise. On July 25, 1864 "Babbage's Bill" became law.

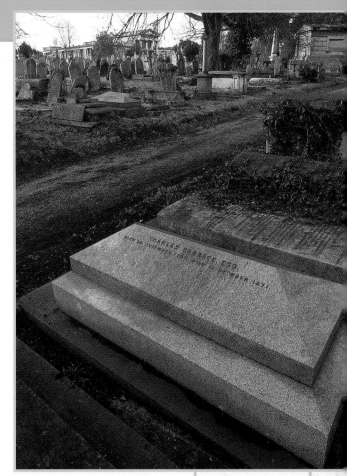

Babbage is buried at Kensal Green in London.

Babbage's death

Charles Babbage died on October 18, 1871. He was almost 80 years old. His funeral was a small affair, and his remains were finally laid to rest in Kensal Green cemetery in London. Had his machines been built, who knows what recognition in terms of fame and maybe even fortune might have been heaped upon him, or how large that final procession to his place of rest might have been?

Maybe the most appropriate words of remembrance come from Joseph Henry of the **Smithsonian Institution**, written shortly after Babbage's death:

"Hundreds of mechanical appliances in the factories and workshops of Europe and America, scores of ingenious expedients in mining and architecture, the construction of bridges and boring tunnels, and a world of tools by which labor is benefited and the arts improved—all the overflowings of a mind so rich that its very waste became valuable to utilize—came from Charles Babbage."

Babbage's Legacy

Babbage designed some of the most complex machines of his day, but not one of them was ever completed. This has been blamed on Babbage's perfectionist personality, disputes with workers and his chief engineer Joseph Clement, poor funding, escalating costs, unhelpful government decisions, and the limitations of machine-tool technology at the time. No doubt each of these reasons contributed, in some way, to the failure to build the machines.

Babbage kept his thoughts and new ideas in his "scribbling books." There are between six and seven thousand pages stored at the Science Museum in London.

Computer lineage

Although Babbage is nicknamed the "Father of the Computer," his work did not lead directly to what we know today as a computer. His machines were based on gears, levers, and moving parts—not on electric circuitry, as today's computers are. His determination to make machines able to calculate, however, inspired many future computer engineers.

The broad legacy

Babbage's true legacy lies elsewhere. He was instrumental in putting science back into a much more central position in society, and he made huge strides in bridging the gap between pure science and applied mechanics. He made people aware that science affects everyone. His book, *On the Economy of Machinery and Manufactures* (1834), had a direct influence on the writing and thoughts of two later 19th-century giants of political economy, John Stuart Mill and Karl Marx.

Babbage's influence and legacy stretch far and wide. In all the areas in which he was actively involved—political, scientific, economic, and social—he brought a forward-looking, modern view. This view was based on his optimistic belief in democracy, **capitalism,** and the ability of the human race to use its creative and analytical mind to overcome practical problems as well as theoretical ones. He foresaw, for example, that one day coal mines might run out. He said that if the great minds of the day could not solve the problem of lack of coal as and when it arose, then the human race deserved to get frostbite!

This British stamp was issued on March 5, 1991 in recognition of Babbage's scientific achievements.

Inventions

Throughout his life, Babbage enjoyed coming up with all kinds of inventions and suggestions. Some were very practical suggestions, such as a carriage in which people could live for a period of time while traveling (like a modern-day camper, it had a stove, toilet, and bed), a tug boat with winching machinery for taking boats against the current, diving bells, and a submarine powered by compressed air. Others concerned the running of the country and the economy, for instance the adoption of decimal currency, a free **market economy,** and abolishing **hereditary peerage** in favor of life peerage. This is an amazingly modern list of inventions and themes—like so many of the things associated with Babbage, they were far ahead of their time.

> *"One of the benefactors of mankind, and one among the noblest and most ingenious sons of England."*
>
> (A tribute to Charles Babbage written by the Swedish mathematicians Georg and Edvard Scheutz in 1857)

43

Timeline

1640s	First calculators made by French philosopher Blaise Pascal.
1789	Storming of Bastille on July 14 marks beginning of French Revolution.
1791	The Babbages move to London. Charles Babbage born, December 26.
1794	Brother Henry born (dies in infancy).
1796	Other brother born (dies in childhood).
1798	Sister Mary Anne Babbage born.
1803	Father Benjamin retires from banking and returns to Totnes, Devon.
1808	Charles suffers a fever and goes to school in Devon.
1810	Begins studies at Trinity College, Cambridge.
1811	Meets Georgiana Whitmore.
1812	Helps found the Analytical Society. Charles and Georgiana Whitmore become engaged.
1813	*Memoirs of the Analytical Society* published.
1814	Charles graduates from Cambridge. Charles and Georgiana Whitmore marry on July 2 in Teignmouth, Devon, and move to London.
1815	Napoleon defeated at the Battle of Waterloo, June 18. Charles and Georgiana's first child born. (Between 1815 and 1827 they had eight children. Only three survived into adulthood.)
1816	Charles becomes a member of the **Royal Society.**
1819	Visits Paris with John Herschel.
1820	Helps set up the Astronomical Society.
1822	Builds first model of a Difference Engine.
1823	Given his first major financial grant from the government.
1826	Charles and Georgiana go to Paris.
1827	Charles's father Benjamin dies, February 27. Charles sends his sons Herschel and Charles to school in London. Georgiana dies in August. Charles goes on a tour of Europe, which lasts a year.
1828	Made Lucasian Professor of Mathematics at Cambridge, a position he held until 1839. He never gave any lectures at the university, though it was expected of him.

1830	King George IV dies, June 26.
	Reflections on the Decline of Science published.
1832	*On the Economy of Machinery and Manufactures* published.
	Reform Bill passed by Parliament.
	Babbage unsuccessfully runs for election in Finsbury, London.
1833	Stops work on the first Difference Engine.
1834	Starts thinking about the Analytical Engine.
	Runs for Parliament and loses again.
	Daughter Georgiana dies.
1843	Son Henry moves to India.
1847–9	Works on the second Difference Engine.
1851	Son Herschel moves to Australia with his family.
1852	Ada Lovelace dies, November 29.
1862	Difference Engine exhibited at the International Exhibition in London.
1864	Charles's autobiography, *Passages from the Life of a Philosopher*, published.
	"Babbage's Bill" passed by Parliament.
1871	Son Henry returns from India to care for his father.
	Charles Babbage dies, October 18, aged 79.

More Books to Read

The Age of Computers. Chicago, Ill.: World Book, Inc., 1998.

Collier, Bruce, and James MacLachlan. *Charles Babbage and the Engines of Perfection.* New York: Oxford University Press, 1999. An older reader can help you with this book.

Hoare, Stephen. *The Digital Revolution.* Austin, Tex.: Raintree Steck-Vaughn Publishers, 1999.

Glossary

Agricultural Revolution huge change in methods of farming that started in Britain in the 18th century and spread to other countries in Europe, as well as the United States

annuity sum of money paid to a person every month or year for a fixed period of time or for their lifetime

aristocrat noble such as a duke or an earl, who owns large areas of land, makes up the highest class in society, and traditionally held political power

bigotry blind attachment or devotion to a particular political party or religion

calculus branch of mathematics developed by Sir Isaac Newton

cam machine part that changes circular movement to movement in a straight line

capitalism economic system in which business and trade operate privately and competitively, with the main goal of making a profit

Chancellor of the Exchequer senior member of the British government who is responsible for the national economy

common land land, such as forests and fields, that people could use free of any charge, to graze their animals and gather any produce that grew there

constituency area where a single member of Parliament may be elected by the people living there

constitution rules that set out how a country should be governed

constitutional monarchy country that has a king or queen as its formal head of state, but which is actually governed by an elected parliament, not by the monarch

cottage industry traditional industry, such as spinning, weaving, or pottery, carried out at home. It was a common way of adding to the family income in the 18th century.

curriculum subjects that are studied in a school

dowry money or property that a bride's family gives to the bridegroom when a couple get married

Enclosure Acts Parliamentary acts that put common land into private ownership and enclosed open fields

gravity force that attracts one object to a larger one. The strength of the force depends upon the object's mass.

Great Reform Bill bill passed by Parliament in London in 1832 that extended voting rights to many men in the growing middle classes

guillotine machine used to execute people by beheading them

hereditary peerage system in which titles and status of noblemen or women are inherited from ancestors

Industrial Revolution sudden growth in mechanical and economic development that began in Britain in the second half of the 18th century, and spread throughout Europe and the United States

International Exhibition exhibition that took place in Europe or the United States, where countries could show off their goods and inventions

lathe machine tool used for turning wood or metal so that it can be worked on

laws of motion Isaac Newton's three scientific laws relating to force in the universe

liberalism political and social system that believes in the maximum amount of freedom and personal liberty, government for the people, abolition of privilege, and the use of some state resources to help the most needy in society

market economy economic system that allows freedom for people to buy what they want, if they can afford it, and for businesspeople to produce the goods to supply them

mayor person who is in charge of a town or city

monarchy country or society that is ruled by a king or queen

precision engineering use of science to design tools that need to be highly accurate and are often quite small

republic country or state whose head is not a king or queen, but a president, elected into that position

Royal Institution organization founded in London in 1799 to support and promote science.

Royal Society most prestigious scientific society in Britain

Smithsonian Institution academic organization founded in 1846 in Washington, D.C., that carries out scientific research

Index

DATE			